LET'S FIND OUT ABOUT
CHRISTMAS

Let's Find Out About

CHRISTMAS

by Franklin Watts
Pictures by Mary Ronin

FRANKLIN WATTS, INC.
575 Lexington Avenue
New York, N.Y. 10022

The author's royalties are donated to the
Frederic G. Melcher Scholarship Fund.

LET'S FIND OUT ABOUT
CHRISTMAS

What is the happiest day of the year?
Most children will say it is Christmas,
December 25th.

It is the day when people say "Merry
   Christmas" to each other.
Boys and girls and grown-ups give gifts
   and get gifts.

They sing songs called Christmas carols.

What is Christmas?

Christmas is the day when people
celebrate the birth of Jesus.
The people who believe that Jesus is the
Son of God call him Christ and are
Christians.

Christians are the family of Jesus Christ.
The word Christmas means *Christ* and
mass.

A mass is said in church.
Many Christians go to church on
Christmas Day.

Christmas comes in the winter.

The trees and plants used at Christmas
are evergreen.

Evergreen plants and trees show that life
goes on all of the time.

A Christmas plant called holly has green
   leaves and red berries.

This is why Christmas colors are red and
   green.

The Christmas tree has evergreen leaves
that are long and pointed like needles.

The "star" at the top of the tree is for the star that men followed to find the place where Jesus was born.

The Christmas flower is called poinsettia,
after a man named Poinsett.

Saint Nicholas is the saint of children.
He first told them to put up a stocking on
the night before Christmas.

The name Santa Claus comes from Saint
   Nicholas.
It is said that Santa Claus carries his bag
   of gifts to give to children who have
   been good all year.

Many people who are not Christians also
give gifts at Christmas.

Small gifts are put in stockings.

Larger gifts are put by the Christmas tree.

A baby may get a rattle.
A girl may get a doll.
A boy may get a book.

Boys and girls and grown-ups send
Christmas cards to friends.

Many give gifts to people in need.

Everyone tries to make other people
   happy at Christmas.
That is why at Christmas we say, "Merry
   Christmas."